Neither Here Nor There

(with a short auto-biography and poem)

By

Michael O'Leary

Earl of Seacliff Art Workshop
Paekakariki 2015

978-1-86942-155-7

1: I am from Irish ancestry on both sides of my family and the Fitzgerald side of the family spent a lot of time around Te Arawa regions, especially Rotorua. This whakatauki is a mixture of two works: the first tells of the importance of knowledge and wisdom as life-affirming aspects of being a human in this world, the second comes from Te Arawa and tells of the natural world, and how we must celebrate both the natural and human worlds in song and dance, and most writers, academic or otherwise, often ask the question: 'How far will my voice and words travel?'

2: The German novelist Günter Grass in his 2007 autobiography *Peeling the Onion* throughout the book often, when talking of the past or trying to evoke accurate memories, will mention 'himself' as 'possibly someone else' or' someone similar' to himself. For example, our Grandmother used to hint at the possibility that we had German ancestry, but there is no evidence of this apart from a memory I had of something she may have said and as this is a memoir that is where it stands.

3: It will be seen that this is also the case with an idea that we may have Māori blood, that there is now no evidence does not deny the fact that I grew up thinking that we had, and this was re-inforced by the fact that during my difficult years in my mid-twenties that it was often my Māori friends, as well as my artist and personal friends, who cared for me and allowed me to feel I was of value before I was reunited with my sister. While Grass may have particular historical reasons for taking this approach I, in my 'Bibel', do not invoke anyone else as I do in my novels, for example. Like Grass, I have no 'record whatsoever of my beginnings'.

3: When our parents died in 1968 all our belongings were burned or otherwise disposed of. I suppose that this was an attempt by our uncle to rid us 'Orākei Bastards' of the perceived taint of
our previous State House, inferior existence, so that 1968 would become our 'Year One'. Sincethen I have hovered between being either a refugee who has lost everything or a Holocaust Survivor who feels the guilt of survival and a Nazi war criminal on the run. [Apocrypha Paipera Aroha: 'What were you this time, a Nazi or a Jew?]

4: Thus, every thought, word, and deed in this book is my own, whether expressed poetically or prosaically and at whatever age or time in my life, but not necessarily recollected in tranquility! Of course, some memories are painful in the extreme, and I try not to hurt others. But, you can't live on this earth for over sixty years and not have done some damage to yourself and others, no matter how unintentionally.

5: The reason I have chosen to call this autobiography 'Die Bibel' is complex, and as is my wont, both serious and humorous. Firstly, the Catholic religion has been a major part of my life, the fact that Catholics are not encouraged to read the Bible is an irony I have often pondered. How can you misinterpret the word of God? You could say the Bible is the book that I've never read that's had the most influence on my life. This can also be taken further into my career as an author, publisher and bookseller, by the fact that the first book published using a printing press was the Gutenberg Bible.

6:   Next, the German word for 'the' is 'die', another ironic twist of language considering how many people 'died' at the hands of German ideologies in the Twentieth Century.

7:   Thirdly, the font I am using for the chapter headings was designed by the famous Kleédinsky and is called 'Bauhaus 93', a tip of the hat to one of the many groups persecuted by the Nazis. Add to this mix the fact that our grandmother who lived with us used to say: 'The love and mercy of God is so great that even Hitler could be in Heaven'.

8:   Several more details of my life and thoughts appear in the 'Apocrypha' section of this memoir. While these are in fact from my novels and prose works published over the last 30 years or so they also add elements of my 'weltanschauung' that not only embellish my existence but are quintessential to understanding me as a person.

9:   Likewise with the poems that appear in the 'Apocrypha' as the 'Psalms' in this work. They often say things about me and my state of being, both at a given time of my life, and also add a further dimension to the thoughts and experiences I am trying to give expression to.

10:   I quote Günter Grass at the beginning of this bible: "nor is there an exercise book of school compositions ... there is no record whatsoever of my beginnings" – this is also true of my life, as will be seen. The same is true of the quote from Jung in that I have carried my mother and father with me through my life.

11:   I remember my son's mother, Aroha, and my Samoan girlfriend, Litia, both telling me in their own ways that I had to let my mother go. The fact that I have not been able to probably explains my inability to form a lasting, loving relationship with any of my lovers. The 'utmost concentration on a goal' that Jung talks of is my life as an 'artist', a lonely and often painful existence, but one that has kept me 'whole' and stopped me from going insane, although that in itself has often nearly tipped me over the brink, as does any great love or passion.

12:   Throughout *Die Bibel* I will often use my poems to illustrate or display some thoughts and feelings which are not able to be explained in prose without killing or inhibiting the original thoughts they give expression to, which is why I wrote them in the first place. My poetry has always been my way of expressing the intangible aspects of my life, especially my love poems.

13:   *Die Bibel* should be read in conjunction with the 2009 book *The Earl is in … 25 Years of the Earl of Seacliff – A to Z* the brilliant work edited by fellow poet and publisher, Mark Pirie, which documents my history as a publisher and bohemian personality in the New Zealand literary and artistic life of New Zealand Aotearoa between 1984 and 2009.

14:   *The Earl is in …* also features several anecdotes and short memoirs relating to me by others in the literary-artistic world which offer insights beyond my own observations and acts as a companion to the present volume. I have refrained from using too many photographs of people that I know and love because the 'who to leave in/who to leave out' aspect, so, except for whānau, I have followed my DADA/ surrealist inclinations when it comes to illustrations.

Michael O'Leary (from his auto-biography, *Die Bibel*)

Rübesahl

a fable with a prologue and epilogue.

Prologue

Meine name ist Rübesahl
For many centuries I lived on the outskirts
Of towns and villages near the Black Forest
And one of my names means Ghost of the Mountains
My dark hair and beard made me mysterious
And people would fear
And revere me
In 1944 I left my ancestral home
Haunted by the darkness and anarchy which reigned

i

I could not travel as a spirit
For the world had made me worldly
By the time I left old Germany
So I escaped in a U Boat wolf-pack

Not used to temporal confinements
And restrictions of the human body
I roamed restless from country to country
Afraid of nothing but my own fears

At nights whilst I wandered some foreign road
The moon and stars shining in my brain
My heart would be reminded of the pain
Caused by loneliness and separation

I carried the burden of guilt for my people
Though no one I met ever knew this
But there was not a woman I could kiss
And not feel that I was a deceiving Judas

ii

At the half-century I arrived as a not born baby
In the remote southern land
Nothing more than an embryo, a bland
Homunculus in my Mother's womb

I arrived early and so
Was a little unsteady on my feet
My understanding of things was incomplete
And education just confused the issue

So with a child's mind I tried
To understand why I didn't belong
Why I felt unusual, why all wrong
Amongst these foreign people, my family

Once I was playing war with other boys
And I wore the symbol of the broken cross
The swastika, I was the Kommandant, the boss
But my father told me off, saying I could be arrested

iii
Later my earth parents died
Other people tried to tie me down
But I felt threatened and thought I would drown
In the sea of human obligation

I moved southward on a journey of discovery
I went to a place which was neither here nor there
It was this strange stone city where
They told me why I didn't belong

One day I stood on a mountain
Snow was falling on the surrounding rocks
The cold went to my bones - a memory unlocks
In my mind, a vision of the Black Forest in winter

Am I evil, I wondered
And this thought drove me on like a demon
The darkness inside me fueled the notion
I moved further away from the life around me

iv
Three women teachers came to me, old and young
Dark and light, friend and lover
With each of them I would discover
Something of myself and my loneliness

One of the three tried to awaken me as a human
You are just ordinary she said to me
For a while it is with you I want to be
But I was afraid of her words and love

The next one was my blood sister
Come on she said lets go brother
To find the ancient land of our father and mother

I hugged her close and said goodbye

On a windswept suburban railway platform
The old woman looked at me and said
Rübesahl, Rübesahl like a voice from the dead
And the past before the past opened up before me

Epilogue
What now for this Rübesahl
Who took on human form so he could live
Only now it is too late to return to the spirit
Rübesahl will die and alone and haunted
With the irony of love following him for eternity
His mind will be his Black Forest now
And he will fear
What he reveres
The mist closes around the Ghost of the Mountain
The mist behind which he hid for all those centuries

"NEITHER HERE NOR THERE"

"Not a very interesting life, is it?" said Richard, slipping on his old and tattered silk dressing gown. Michael pondered the statement, rolling it around in his mind like brandy in a barrel. "And I'm a pretty boring sort of fellow" he thought to himself. Richard watched the slow. Imbecilic grin grow, bloom and wilt and thought "It wasn't that funny!" Richard was always irritable this early in the morning and the least trifle could upset his equilibrium at five minute intervals for the following two hours.

Today was their big day. They both had one big day a week which was, without fail, the same day for both of them. It was a day which neither could do without and it produced such traumatic and extreme behaviour in them, both physical and psychological (the spiritual realm shall not be dealt with in this treatise as it is equally abhorrent to both protagonists, and as their biographer I feel as though I would be held responsible for resultant reprisals on the reader – I should then be found responsible for resultant reprisals on the reader – I should then be found guilty by a public court which would make the trial of Heinrich Himmler seem like one for petty theft) that all their friends knew to keep well away until the midnight celebration which was held at the end of every such day if they survived which they always had so far.

It's eleven o'clock and here is the news Today President Sadat "…Had an erection!" Richard's voice blended in with that of the news' reader's so convincingly that Michael who had spent the last quarter of an hour on a philosophical problem encountered whilst tying up his shoe-laces, suddenly leapt to his legs and in a resounding jubilant baritone said "Did you hear that". Richard gave him a quick furtive glance and grimaced as he answered, "What's up!" to Michael. "Sadat's had an erection! It said so on the news! Didn't you hear it!" "How?" Richard said, with a sense of subdued glee, being careful not to look his friend in the eye. "What do you mean how?" In the usual way, I imagine! They didn't say." "He probably brought himself to it – all Arabs are a pack of wankers" said Richard, with a Jewish bent, beginning to laugh openly now.

"Anyway, continued Michael excitedly, "that's not the point. What I'm taken by is that they actually said it on the radio, - Erection!" Michael had become quiet – almost abstract, "Erection, they said erection on the National programme and shortwaves service of Radio New Zealand." He was staring off into space for several minutes while Richard was rolling on the floor with tears of laughter streaming down his young face. After a while his reality forced itself into Michael's trance-like state by its sheer physical weight of sound.

Michael looked at his friend with disgust. "Puerile, vile creature, no sense of guilt or culture" he muttered to himself, and turning away had a sudden retinal encounter with the clock on the mantlepiece and gave a start. "Holy Christ, saviour of the world and other planets, it's 11.15 a.m. If we don't hurry we will miss the bus and thus our appointments with the esteemed Labour Department and out lives will be in ruin." "Pus!" hissed Richard who had picked up the heap of rubble, which was himself, off the floor.

Both men looked at each other, and all antipathy vanished as they realised they had to once more cope with their common problem. This brought each of them to a state of frigidity no woman could match. They stood frozen, both felt as though they were made of wood which had been left in the refrigerator for some suburban family's pet termite; that is, terror had struck! I shall not explain all the nuances involved in their malaise.

Suffice it to say that when either or both decided to go out of their dwelling on their own accord or were forced out by some form of coercion such as the present, they were seized by a terrible and unaccountable fear, which was simply this: Neither knew when they stepped outside into the repulsive rays of sunlight which distinguished day from night, whether they would be stepping into the streets of Auckland or the streets of Dunedin.

Were they in Ponsonby or Normanby; were they in Herne Bay or St Clair. Were they in Karangahape Road or George Street; were they in Symonds Street or Princess Street; Anzac Avenue or Anzac Avenue, etc … Their dilemma intensified as the seconds rushed by and their bus drew nearer to the stop at which they alighted. Their appointment was at 12.30 p.m., their bus left at 11.45 a.m. This left exactly one quarter of an hour to dress, shave, wash and run. So, as usual, they did.

They burst from inside to outside, slammed the door and then raced the bus in the hundred metres dash to the bus stop. Although the vehicle was of the vintage trolley-bus era it managed to beat its human vintage counter-parts and it was only the usual chance that someone was already waiting at the stop which made it possible for the degenerate duo to leap on to the conveyance just as it was leaving. Michael was the first on board, thus avoiding the humiliation and embarrassment which would follow as soon as Richard would get on.

The torture which follows the total blank experienced in the mind which follows the hapless words, "I would like two to ….Two to where? To the exchange or the Civic Centre; two to the Octagon or to Customs Street; two to High Street or to High Street …Where to?" repeated the driver becoming somewhat irate at the dumbfounded expressions on the faces of his two passengers. Suddenly Michael's face lit up like the firmament and he pulled eighty cents from his pocket, handed it to the astounded driver and said in an extremely confident audible voice, "Two to the city!"

CHAPTER II

Julie strolled leisurely down the road which led from her home to the railway station. She had at least ten minutes to walk the final hundred yards or so and it was a beautiful spring afternoon. All the gardens of suburban Johnsonville had a bright colourful atmosphere despite the dreary mentality of the people who had laid them. The train had not yet arrived at the Johnsonville Station as she crossed the tracks and walked along the platform.

There were not many people waiting to catch the unit back to Wellington: a few shift workers from the state-housing areas who would go into Wellington and wait for another train to take them to some god-forsaken factory up the Hutt Valley. Julia mused, almost brooded, on this point. She was thinking what hard lives some people must have when the train arrived and broke her whimsical contemplation.

"Good afternoon, Julie," said Mr Johnson, as he stepped on the platform. "Oh! Good afternoon, Mr Johnson. Have you had a good day?" said Julie as she realised where she was. "Nothing too strenuous," replied Mr Johnson, "and where are you off to?" Julie looked at her next door neighbour with an air of disbelief and then said quickly, "I'm going to visit friends in another part of the country. I'll be away for a few days so I've fixed up with Mrs Johnson to feed the cats." "Fine", replied Mr Johnson. "Good-by; and have a good trip." "Thank you, I will", she said.

Julie watched Mr Johnson, with affectionate amusement as he walked slowly down the platform, and his dark, well-pressed suit, his bowler hat, and his umbrella reminded her of Richard's first reaction to her aged penguin-like friend. He had been staying with her whilst in transit between Auckland and Dunedin or vice-versa (she could never remember which) and after he had been introduced to her neighbour he sat down later that evening and wrote a very funny, satirical short story which he called; "Johnson of Johnsonville: a definitive history of a civil servant with a past".

As Julie boarded the 3.15 p.m. train she remembered her mock-anger as she chastised Richard for making fun of such a lovely old man. Richard had taken amoral stance and the story was so good and he was so beautiful and incorrigible that she had to forgive him his follies. As the train pulled away from the station she gave a sudden start. Her feelings were at once excited and apprehensive. She had not seen Richard for nearly two months and she could not help keep wondering if he had changed and how, and how they would react to each other.

They had been together for nearly two years and had broken up at the beginning of the year because he did not want to move to Wellington. She had moved there because of her job with television and apart from that one time when he had stayed for a week during transit between the two poles which governed his existence, they had not seen each other for eight or nine months.

As the train left Ngaio Station Julie looked once more at the telegram which had arrived shortly after 2.30 p.m.

"Julie dear. We both received a large sum of back-pay from the dole office about half-an-hour ago and are having a party tonight. Go to airport and pick up your ticket before 6.30 p.m. It is paid for stop./Go./The plane leaves Wello at 7p.m./stop. We had better stop here/stop/as this telegram has already cost over a thousand dollars stop/stop/stop/Love Michael and Richard"

Julie laughed aloud and the few other passengers looked at her and then looked quickly away as she turned and realised where she was. She felt embarrassed despite herself and was annnoyed that she could not enjoy herself openly in public. "What a pack of morons" she thought harshly and then she felt remorse for thinking so badly of others and so on until at last she brought this line of thought to a close by saying to herself, "Richard is right! I am just an ordinary New Zealander with all the resultant hang-ups! She felt both bemused and sad at this thought and to avoid thinking anymore at the moment she turned and looked out of the window of the train.

The train had just emerged from the last tunnel on the line and was now clanking over the viaduct which took it across the worm-like motorway which was gradually eating its way through the core of the capital city. Julie had caught a glimpse of Oriental Bay and the surrounding hills on which the late afternoon sun shone harsh and oblique. Wellington seemed hard-edged and gold-tinted on one side and dark, sumptuous and sombre on the other and Julie thought of a golden Inca temple-city which had been liberated from hundreds of years of rubble – half beauty and half decay.

The train was now entwined in a mass of rails and points, lights of green, red, and amber shone at the places where rails ran into one another. As the unit pulled into Wellington Central Railway Station, Julie could see the people on the outside waiting with tired, anxious faces and weary, sagging bodies burdened down with parcels, satchels, and all manner of paraphernalia, just dying to get into their mobile cocoons which would then whisk them homeward. Julie always felt guilty because she had a job which allowed her to take time off whenever she wanted, was well-paid and interesting. As she got out of her carriage she thought, "One day I'll get a 'real' job," and then, "Only joking" and crossed her fingers.

It was 6.05 p.m. by the time the bus reached the airport terminus. Between getting off the train or on the bus, Julie had been to say goodby to Cheryl and was feeling really good. She walked straight up to the ticket counter and collected her ticket. She then sat down, lit a cigarette and read he newspaper until her flight number was called.

She was in the middle of an article on the future of the Middle-East when a woman's voice called over the speaker. "Attention! Attention! Flight 614 for Auckland and Flight 710 for Dunedin. All aboard please. Passengers for Flight 614 go through gate 2 and for Flight 710 through gate 4. Thank you."

Julie put her newspaper in her bag and stood up. She was motionless in thought for a few seconds and then walked off quickly through the gate to her plane.

CHAPTER III

Michael and Richard leapt off the trolley-bus and headed home. They looked like two large bats as they sped along the footpath – their movements were filled with a sense of urgency, their long black coats flying out like capes. They walked with their eyes downwards in order to avoid seeing the street names which stuck out so tantalisingly from what seemed like each lamp-post.

The reason why they so religiously ignored, what might seem to an outsider, the most obvious and immediate solution to their twin-city schizophrenic problem was that they had tried it once and it had created more chaos than ever. It was during the particularly cold winter of 197…when they both refused to go abroad even to the local dairy. The telephone and Julie were their only communication with the outside world and it was through these media that all provisions, needs and wants were attended to.

In July or August of 197…they had become so intent on finding out which city they were in that it had become an obsession. So one day they sent Julie out to solve once and for all this hitherto insoluble dilemma. She was sensible and could no doubt conclude the matter one way or the other. Julie went to the corner store and brought a newspaper. On her way home a light snow shower fell. She ran, reaching home almost in an ecstasy, burst through the door, threw the paper on the floor and, after catching her breath told Richard and Michael of the snow.

Michael cried, "We must be in Dunedin!" Richard was about to give Michael a triumphant embrace (both had agreed from the start that their relationship would have the barest amount of physical contact, reserved for special occasions when they triumphed over the world together. For, although the loved the "poetic element" in each other, they both repulsed each other physically, in the extreme) when his wayward glance happened upon the headlines of the newspaper which lay open at the front page by his feet.

Richard, with a sharp gesture, repulsed his friend's open arms, and fell, moaning like a sick animal, to the couch. Michael, at first taken aback, then much alarmed, looked at Julie for an insight into what he should do. She went over to Richard and asked him what was wrong. Both she and Michael had no trouble in comprehending what had sent their friend into such anguish after Richard had pointed them towards the headlines of the paper. It was not the large type which read "Coldest winter in New Zealand's history " that took the tongues out of their heads but a smaller headline, "Snow falls on Ponsonby: first time for fifty years".

Julie went over to Richard and slowly nursed him back to a state in which he was able to see the door slam behind Michael. "Where's he going?" Richard shouted. He brooded briefly, thinking where his friend might have gone. "Michael has not been outside for two or three months" he thought. "He could come to grief." Suddenly he turned panic-stricken to Julie and screamed, "He's imitating Oliver Reed. Oh! My God!" and an image of Michael wandering off alone to his death in the snows of Mount Cargill or One Tree Hill or wherever the fucking hell they were flashed across his unbalanced mind. He lay motionless: impotent and listless he mumbled things to himself: inaudible noises which Julie could not decipher. Sweat poured off his bumpy forehead.

Michael wandered through the decaying part of the city past derelict houses and disused shops and factories. It was a small area in relation to the greater area of the city but it was the part he knew and loved. He had few human attachments, so his emotional outlets were satisfied in the main by the parts of Dunedin and Auckland which had long ago been deserted by decent folk.

The parts where the students, migrant workers, and poorer natives lived, or else those which the authorities had ear-marked for urban renewal in more affluent times, and could now not even afford to demolish let alone rebuild. There was a slight snow falling, mixed with drizzle and night was descending like a large dark velvet curtain. Lights were being turned on everywhere and the whole atmosphere appeared to Michael like a surrealistic field of mushrooms springing up to meet the night. However, on this occasion his mission was stronger than his melancholia. He was going to look at street names and he would do this by seeking out likely lamp-posts as a dog might. The difference between him and his canine counterpart would be simple and unambiguous. Whereas a dog would surely tilt a back leg to 45° angle on making the desired encounter, he would tilt his head on the angle of 45° in order to read the street and thus solve the mystery previously mentioned.

"Such is the sublime difference between man and beast" mused Michael. Then turning to his business he wandered on, head down, deep in thought. He walked for about a mile, past many lamp-posts. He was so absorbed in preoccupation he forgot to make the necessary angular tilt.

In his mind he was trying to collate all the information his brain had stored on the subject he had asked it about which was! "Could you please tell me the names of the streets in Auckland from roughly the area border by Karangahape Road, Ponsonby Road, College Hill and Queen Street which correlate with the street names in Dunedin found in the area roughly bordered by Stuart Street, Anzac Avenue, Dundas Street, Duke Street and Queen Street.

Soon the answers flowed in, and Michael thought, "If I can find out all the streets of the same nomenclature in the two areas, when I finally come to street with a different name all I have to do is see which city it's in, and I will have a certain knowledge of where we are in. He became progressively excited as the street names flowed from his brain. Smith, Brown, Howe, Russell, Scotland, Union, London, Pitt, Harbour, Queen.

As the definite flow came to a halt Michael found himself leaning against a lamp-post. Beads of sweat had settled on his brows. He knew the moment of truth had come. The age of reason had been reached and he must live with and use the knowledge he was about to receive. He became calm and without further hesitation he took two steps away from the pole and prepared for the upward tilt which would free him from bondage.

His initial inclination had been to carry out the necessary movement of the cranium case as quickly as possible, thus enabling him to find out the street name, then deduce the identity of their particular whereabouts all in a matter of seconds. However, the significance of the event was so overwhelming, he thought not only was it impossible for his blood pressure to cope with such enlightenment, but also that some sense of style might be considered by so civilized a patron of the earth as himself.

The odyssey began! Head tilted 45° South up and the first letter appeared before him. M. He moved on to the next with cautious confidence, as a baby takes its second step. A. These were definitely new letters. Neither had been mentioned in conjunction with the other in the cor-relative list. Third letter, C. had his mind racing. Almost convinced of victory he read the fourth letter almost carelessly. K. He was now convinced!

It must be MacKelvie Street, Grey Lynn. So sure was he of his vision he almost forgot to stay and read the remaining letters. He paused briefly to collect his happily scattered thoughts; onward he thought, with conviction. The next letter was E and for poor Michael it may have been a machine-gun held two inched from his head. He could not, of course, go on now.

His remembrance of a street called Mackenzie not far from the botanical gardens in Dunedin North made the situation beyond his powers of redemption. Blinded by confusion he ran reaching Richard and Julie and their home, shattered. Both he and Richard thenceforth agreed to study lamp-posts as a means of solving their precise and tormenting problem. "It seems as though the attempted solution is ten times worse than the projected disease" said Richard later that evening, and the incident was never talked of again, but left to fester and rot malignantly in both their minds.

Richard shuddered violently as he was brought back to the present by Michael's voice asking if he had the key. "What??? Oh yes! The key! Yes I do have the key, the good old key" he said, assuming an air of abandonment as he tried to forget the memories he had so unwittingly been engrossed in during their mad dash for home. However, Richard remained so distracted that when a telegram arrived about 7.30 p.m. saying "Arriving tonight about 9.30 Love Julie" he became alarmed and immediately asked a puzzled Michael his views on why she might be coming. Michael threw his arms in the air as a gesture of despair-cum-disdain, and went off to the bedroom for a rest.

Michael moved quickly along the narrow canyon, walked in by shops that was Karangahape Road. It was a late shopping night and people were rushing with baskets and children. Michael did not look anyone in the eye for fear of giving away his secret. When he reached St Kevin's Arcade he stood for a few seconds at the corner, to check if he was being followed. He looked up and down the long, snake-like road. On each corner an S.S. guard stood, their black demonic uniforms stood out against the well-lit streets and colourful clothes of the Polynesian people. Karangahape Road was a world unto itself and could still appear as though it were mid-day even though it may be midnight. Even the Nazi occupation had not out a damper on this festival of colour and light!

Taking a last glance Michael satisfied himself that all was in order and took a head-long dive down the steps which led to Myers Park. At the bottom of these steps in the Arcade he cam to a door on his right. No. 4 was the flat he wanted. He gave the secret knock, and with a certain amount of suspicion the old Jew at the entrance let him past and locked the door behind him.

The room he was led into was smoke-filled and dimly-lit. There were about thirty or forty Jewish men and women. A meeting was in progress and much emotional language was used, and many people were crying or slightly sobbing. The old man who had let Michael in raised his hand and once everyone had become silent indicated to Michael that he should speak.

Michael moved to the centre of the room and in a low, hesitant voice said, "They've arrested Richard". Everyone was stunned and stared in disbelief at this stranger who bore them such devastating news. After a while a tall man with a long beard and Jewish priest's hat came forward and said to Michael, "I have seen you before, but many here have not. Perhaps you could explain your friendship with Richard and how you know of his fate."

Michael was about to speak when there was a loud banging on the outside door. All the Jewish inhabitants of the room froze. Before they had time to panic or act the door was broken down and the room was filled with the black-death plague of twenty-five S.S. men.

Everyone was rounded up and pushed against the far wall of the room. The soldiers formed a line of a firing squad and raised their machine-guns in preparation to shoot.

Five minutes passed and the hostages were in a prolonged state of terror and confusion: each wondered why they were still alive. Michael felt singularly odd. He had never been in the front-line of a firing squad before. He was thinking about Richard and the events of the day when his thoughts were interrupted by the entry of Gala Day.

Obergruppenfuerher Gala Day was an altogether strange and bizarre character. Instead of the usual black S.S. uniform he wore a pure white one. This was covered by insignia, medals and embroidery of many bright colours, yellow, red, blue, green, etc. He looked like the personification of a spring garden on a sunny day. He gave a cynical smile as he said, "Guten Tag, Mein Juden Freund". Michael looked at the person who was known as "the laughing butcher" and remembered with self-hatred the deal he had contracted in order to save Richard's life.

Gala Day walked over to him and said, "Hello my friend, you have done well" and with a sharp gesture to one of the guards at the door a badly beaten body was thrown into the middle of the room. Herr Gala Day continued, a cruel smile on his handsome face, "However, as you can see, due to our very strick theories on race we could not let even one Jew live. Unfortunately, there is no such things as rehabilitation of the blood." Gala Day turned to his S.S. soldiers and said, "FIRE!"

After ten minutes of fanatical machine-gun fire, all the people lay in each other's blood but Michael was still alive. Sent into an ocean of remorse he was screaming as Gala Day and his men left. He screamed. "Shoot me!" Michael was on his knees shaking violently "Shoot me! Shoot me!"

Michael finally heard Richard saying, "Wake up! I haven't got a gun" and felt Richard shaking him. Michael took a while to recognise the familiar surroundings of their room. When he was back to reality he was told by his friend that it was just after 9 p.m. and they still had quite a lot to do to organise for the party. Michael explained to

Richard that he had another Nazi dream. Richard grimaced and asked him, "What were you this time: a Nazi or a Jew?"

CHAPTER IV

After spending about half an hour trying to avoid talking to a young businessman sitting next to her in the plane, Julie finally succeeded and she looked out the window and fell deep into thought. She did not like travelling by air, because she usually met creeps of businessmen who always tried to chat her up and also she could never believe or comprehend a journey which took about 12 or 15 hours by rail or road could be made in half an hour.

Also the height at which these aircraft flew made her feel vulnerable. She couldn't understand why she could survive so far from the earth whilst travelling at such a speed. It was like trying to think of God or death, one could rationalise for so long then leave the rest to chance.

She tried to think of things or problems which were more tangible and more readily resolved. Richard was the first and most complex in the hierarchy of this lower category of thoughts. Julie mused that he was like a bridge between thinking about the mystery of the blessed Virgin and what one was going to have for dinner.

Michael inevitably occurred to her simultaneously as Richard came into her mind. She had known Michael first an had gone out with him quite a few times. They used to talk a lot together and were very close in a "mystical" way. He understood a lot about people and especially women. This meant he had a lot of close female friends but never had girl friends or lovers. At the time Julie met Richard (he and Michael who had known each other for quite a while, were as close as two male friends could be) she and Michael had almost reached an agreement to become unofficially engaged.
One night she and Michael were around at his place and he mentioned that one of his friends from the North Island was coming to stay with him in Dunedin for about a week.

That night Richard arrived off the railcar from Christchurch and when he and Julie met the next day both knew that something immediate and irrevocable had happened inside each of them. They kept their meetings secret for about a week but Michael was aware that something was afoot and pressed the point one evening. The three of them got into a fierce argument which ended in Michael putting his coat and hat on and leaving. They didn't see or hear from him until they received a telegram from Auckland a week later sating. "Join me in the big A when possible. All is forgiven. Love. Michael."

"Would you like a sweet to chew on, we will be landing soon," said the hostess, as she passed a large tray of assorted lollies across the young businessman towards Julie. "Uh? Oh! I'm sorry I was away in a dream" said Julie. 'Yes. I'd love one please?"

"Not too long now" said her boringly well-groomed neighbour, in a manner which she had become well-aquainted with and which she despised.

"No? How long exactly?" she asked politely, almost thankful for a small dose of trivia to take her away from her own dark-edge thoughts.

"About five minutes" he replied eagerly, pleased at this sudden revival of communication with his attractive fellow-traveller. However his pleasure was short-lived, for as he turned to resume his former intimacy, he found her in the abstracted attitude which she had been in for the previous twenty minutes.

Julie went through a wide variety of feelings including guilt, adventure, remorse, jealousy, etc. Whenever she thought of either Richard or Michael, and there was no time when she thought of them more often or more intensely than just before she was due to see either or both of them again. "In an hour or so I will be with them" she thought amidst feelings of anxiety, joy and anticipation. "Oh how much I still love Richard" she almost talked aloud but her thoughts were interrupted by the loud speaker.

"This is your captain speaking. We are now approaching ..." when she heard the word her heart stood still. She couldn't believe her ears!
She didn't know what to do! She fumbled in her bag for her ticket. Perhaps she had heard the man's voice wrongly. "Yes. That's it, I wasn't listening properly." Her reprieve however, was short-lived.

One glance at the destination confirmed her fears. "Those stupid bastards" she muttered angrily to herself.

"What?" enquired the young man.

"Nothing!" she retorted in such a manner as to leave no doubt that their communication was terminated.

As the jet taxied to a standstill Julie felt suddenly exhausted and exasperated. She gathered her things indifferently and passed the smiling stewardess who was saying, "I hope you had a pleasant journey," as though she didn't exist. By the time she reached the terminal buildings she was feeling slightly more composed and realised that she had to find a telephone. Firstly she would send those two bloody idiots a telegram to say she couldn't make it to the party because they had given her a fucking ticket that sent her four hundred or so miles in the wrong direction: secondly she would have to ring friends in the city to see of she could stay he night.

CHAPTER V

"I wonder where Julie's got to" said Michael. "Her flight got in about two hours ago." Richard was talking with the first arrivals at the party and didn't hear Michael's words, only his voice. "What?" said Richard.

Before Michael could repeat himself he was distracted by a knock at the door. "I'll get it." He said, thinking to himself that it was rather odd, "People don't knock on the door they just open it," and "too early for the police" he mused as he opened the door.

"Richard!" he called anxiously, "a telegram"

Richard broke off from his friends and hurried over to the door. "Well open it! Quickly!" he shouted. Michael clumsily pulled at the envelope. "Don't rip it!" said Richard frantically, (any hint of danger triggered off immediate panic reactions in both of them which increased ten-fold as each second passed). Both read the message.

"Dear fools stop. You have sent me to the wrong city stop by accident and incompetence. I hope stop I will be staying at Joans in Union Street stop Reluctant Love Julie."

Michael and Richard looked at each other embarrassedly, went white in the faces, were silent and stood for about two minutes, looked at the walls, floor and ceiling, and finally looked each other directly in the eye again and simultaneously burst into a fit of uncontrollable laughter. This was their usual response to any emotional trauma whether it be suspension from the dole of the death of a friend.

After a while they reached a state of elegant equilibrium and thus resumed their roles as hosts, seemingly purged, by a complex system of well-rehearsed hysterics, of the guilt inherent in their gross crime of negligence. Julie had been wronged but life must go on, and so must the party. Who were they to destroy the impending pleasure of the myriads of people, including a few friends, who waited all week for their party. How dare either of them think that just because they felt remorseful and should be kneeling on a wooden floor banging their foreheads at regular intervals with a hard-covered edition of the Bible or the Koran, that they could neglect their individual and collective duties to their guests. After all, it is the modern world and the utilitarian principle must rule!

About twenty people had arrived by the time their trauma had ended. Irish whiskey had been designated the drink of the evening and so far there was about three quarters of a bottle average for each drinking guest. Michael picked up the nearest bottle and pondered the inevitable self- destruction involved if such liquor passed his lips. Having reached some decision he said, "Enough!" and took a large swig from the bottle.

Richard, sensing his friend's mood, felt a certain twinge of guilt but realising the impossibility of remedial action grabbed the nearest bottle of Tulamore Dew and drank as though it were mothers milk. Soon they were both on the road to becoming social animals, two introverted worms turning into beautiful, witty butterflies for a one-night stand and fall.

It was now about half an hour after pub-closing time and the swell of people into the small house had become overwhelming. Dozens of fragments chipped form the solid block of humanity were scattered, stumbling and moaning, laughing and frantic, about the few rooms in all manner of poses and positions. Each person jostling and hustling, arriving and innocently looking and hoping to find his or her place in the light of the fifty watt light bulb.

Destiny and fate and any number of philosophical viewpoints (lubricated) by alcohol and drugs and many splendid things, were combining to form a new galaxy, a microcosm of universal proportion. A world-view was forming, one which had never previously existed, a unique entity in which each person participated, oblivious to, and yet an integral part of the individual events and ideas, occurrences and utterances: but although asleep to particulars each person was aware of an overall significance, an underlying sense of collective consciousness, which none could understand if called upon to annunciate, but which was, nonetheless, felt with intensity of the strongest passion.

Drunk and melancholy Richard left the party and walked the city streets, barely aware of anything apart from an overwhelming sadness and disillusionment with himself and thus the whole of humanity. Even vague contemplation of his relationship with the universe did not humble or console him and as he wandered aimlessly on he began to think of the fog which was low and thick as a personification of his limited life and knowledge and his heart sank deeper and deeper.

He had walked for nearly ten minutes engrossed in his personal depression when he chanced upon a lamp-post with a street name plate attached. "Dundas Street" the name registered in his mind like a dull memory and he muttered exhaustedly to himself, "So it is Dunedin" and fell silent.

He crossed the Leith Bridge and began the assent to the brow of the hill which was marked by Clyde Street on his right and Lovelock Avenue on his left. A solitary car passed which he cursed for its intrusion in his painful peace. When he reached the two toads running off Dundas Street he stopped and pondered his immediate future fate. If he went backwards he would be doing what most repelled him after physical contact: that is he would be taking step backwards.

If he went forwards it would mean he would just wander on through the streets of Dunedin with the same purposelessness with which he had pursued the occupation till now, so that going forwards would amount to nothing more than going backwards in the opposite direction there was nothing he resented more than the ironies of nature playing their inexorable tricks on him, although he delighted in their workings on others. If he went to Clyde Street he could visit a friend but that would be cheating and cowardly-defying the indifference of nature with the warmth of friendship was, to Richard, the ultimate side-0step of the existential dilemma, a first-resort and thus a surrender of all principles that were scared.

His final choice lay in the upward path to the Northern Cemetery: Dunedin is the only city in New Zealand with a stereo system for its dead. It would appear to an astute outsider, sat someone from Oamaru, that the living heart of Dunedin, the city, was flanked and amplified by its two main cemeteries, Northern and Southern. Both are situated in places of such significance that few people except those who live in Dunedin, could fail to recognise the metaphorical significance.

So, like so many aspects of this Scot-Goth city, the dullness of its present generation of citizens is matched only by the ironic brilliance and foresight of past generations. And so, with the aid of logic, Richard turned to the left and ascended slowly into the thickness of the mist and fog of Lovelock Avenue. After five minutes walking he reached the gates of the graveyard and stood transfixed for several moments.

Eventually he entered through the straight, ominous gates. Everything had an ethereal air about it. The tombstones stood almost unseen like rocks in murky water. Richard felt that he was some ancient fish swimming through the ruins of some neglected Atlantis. The further he moved away from the outer perimeter of the cemetery the stronger he felt pulled towards its centre. He gathered momentum as some unseen force pulled him with magnetic strength through the city of the dead. He no longer was aware of himself but only existed as a movement. He had no control or perception, rather he was directed by a supernatural agent so that he had become spirit.

In this form he could only feel that he was being moved or maneuvered through objects and over objects which merged and seemed to lose their material life. Faster and faster his life-force flowed until he felt like the wind, swift and unseen, blowing and swirling round and round and up and down and everywhere and anywhere. Just when he felt without fear, that he might lose his existence altogether and evaporate into nothingness his curious movements stopped and Richard fell, exhausted and weak, to the ground.

He lay thus for several minutes, almost asleep, until his glance chanced upon a figure, barely discernible in the fog and darkness, standing not twenty feet from him. With a great effort he got himself up off the ground and stood limply against a crumbling headstone. The figure before him did not move and although his senses were returning Richard could not see it any clearer than before, such was the density of the weather and darkness. As he gained in strength he decided to approach the apparition. Silently he moved forward, his senses alert, his reflexes on the ready.

Closer and closer he moved and only slowly did any discernible human features reveal themselves. He saw that the figure was naked and that it was a woman's body. Long hair fell over her breasts and she was standing upright. He tried to speak but words had left him long ago, so he moved very slowly forward. As he got within arm's length of the person in front of him he had a sudden realisation and his heart almost leapt out of his mouth.

He gave a loud exclamation of bewildered joy and then just as suddenly became as deathly quiet. "Julie", he said in a whisper. The figure did not respond in any way so Richard reiterated, "Julie" slightly more forcefully this time. Still no reaction, so with much hesitancy Richard moved forward and touched his beautiful, misplaced lover. As his hand moved around her shoulder he had the oddest sensation.

He found that this Julie of his was two dimensional. After his first bewildered realisation he examined her closer and sure enough, here was a life-sized cardboard cut-out, complete with backing stand, of his beloved Julie. He wanted to laugh and he wanted to cry, he was violent and helpless, amused and confused.

At this point Richard woke up from his dream and felt an acute-sense of disorientation as well as the most outrageous hangover headache he had ever experienced. Half-remembering his dream, and half-remembering the nightmares of the party the previous night, he stumbled out of his bed with the idea of making a good strong cup of hot, black coffee. At that moment he heard an agonised groan come from the depths that was Michael's bed.

www.ingramcontent.com/pod-product-compliance
Lightning Source LLC
Chambersburg PA
CBHW071231130626
46555CB00004B/1940